UNDERSTANDING THE

CONCEPT

&

BENEFITS

OF BEING

BORN AGAIN

GEORGE ARKHURST

Published by Gloripub
Printed in the U.S.A
Copyright © 2017 George Arkhurst

Request for information should be addressed to:
http://www.gloripub.com

ISBN-13: 978-0997621334
ISBN-10: 0997621338

Dedication

This book is dedicated to my beloved darling wife, Fatmata, and my awesome children, Fanta, Cassandra, Sade, and George Jr.

****

Acknowledgments

****

God Almighty who had done marvelously well, guiding me through life as a whole and with this writing in particular. My parents: the late Mr. Jerry Kwesi Arkhurst and Mrs. Cassandra Arkhurst. My Pastor, Benjamin Boakye, head pastor of Ebenezer Assembly of God church, Bronx, NY; for his support and his willingness to help me greatly in ministry. My able boss and Sunday School superintendent, Minister James Mensah, whose steps I am following in writing and who acted as one of my editors. He did a fine job at that. To my brother, my friend the one and only Minister Tony Aghamiogie, whose helping hand in editing helped refine the end product of the manuscript. My Bro, General Eric Asiedu, who systematically looked over my work and made recommendations to get the most out of this book. To a stranger I met in the Metro North train, Shoshana, who edited a portion of the manuscript during the short trip from Grand Central Station to Stamford. To my sister, Priscilla Sam, who I called Editor in Chief. She painstakingly ran through the final product, refined it putting the last touch making this book a masterpiece. Finally, to every single one of my brothers and sisters in Christ, and to all my friends and well-wishers, I say a big thank you and God richly bless you all.

Contents

Preface

"Truly, truly, I say to you, unless one is born again he cannot see the kingdom of God." John 3.3 (Esv).

"Born again." What does it really mean? Why was it necessary for Jesus to say those words? What is the significance of it? Why should everyone understand the meaning of it? And what had that phrase done since it was said about two thousand years ago?

The term "born again" was heard for the first time when a Jewish religious leader called Nicodemus went to visit Jesus one night. This Nicodemus was a devoted religious man. One who wanted to live a decent moral life in this world; and to get to heaven in the life after. He was also a member of the Jewish ruling council; this council was opposed to the teachings and ministry of Jesus. They had constantly battled Jesus over what is the truth ever since He began His ministry.

Nicodemus a devout member of this group found himself at cross roads in his heart. He saw truth and clarity from what he had heard from Jesus. And this clarity he had not found in his own religious doctrines. He was no longer certain of what to believe. He was in an era that is similar to ours today, where there are different religions with multiple sects and a variation of beliefs. All proclaiming to be the way to God. That bothered Nicodemus, so he went to see Jesus for some enlightenment. He had closely observed Jesus and saw something in Him he had never seen or read about in other religious leaders.

He saw a gracefulness and authority that has never being demonstrated by any of the prophets or priests before Jesus. He knew if anyone would have answers to life's questions it would be Him. So Nicodemus left his house and went to Jesus. Jesus welcomed him and they started a conversation. Nicodemus started to testify of what he had seen in Jesus, expressed his faith in him. He said Jesus was a teacher from God because of what Jesus was doing. As he was speaking Jesus said to him: *"Truly, truly I say to you, unless one is born again he cannot see the kingdom of God."* John 3:3 (ESV) In that sentence, Jesus was saying, Nicodemus, I know why you are here. You want to know what a person can do to gain the kingdom of God. You are interested in the life hereafter. Here is the answer to that, *"...you must be born again"*. Nicodemus did not understand what Jesus meant by that he was confused.

As this term confused Nicodemus in the past, so it has confused the rest of the world even to this day and age. So what does it mean to be born again and how can one be? Nicodemus was vast in the laws of God and was a very religious man but he stood dumbfounded at the words Jesus spoke to him.

This question of how a man can be born again has lingered from that time till now. People of all works of life, religious and non-religious alike have attached meanings to it. Are they holding the right views of the meaning? So what does it really mean to be "born again?" The intent of this book is to do a systematic study to enable us to understand what it means to be born again.

****

ONE

You Must Be Born Again

****

Jesus replied, "Very truly I tell you, no one can see the kingdom of God unless they are born again." John. 3:3

Examining the word "again" in a phrase, indicates that, that particular thing had happened at least once in the past. So when Jesus said we must be "born again" it holds true that we have had that particular type of birth once before. So what birth was Jesus referring to. As humans, we are only familiar with the physical birth. That statement got Nicodemus baffled, I am picturing a jaw dropping moment when he heard that. He could not figure out what that meant. He had gone to inquire of the Lord about how people can possibly gain the kingdom of God. Even though, he was a religious man who had climb the ranks amongst his peers; he did not know how to get to God's kingdom. This had been the reason why he was into religion in the first place. But despite his commitment he knew there was something he was missing. I believe Nicodemus on many occasions has heard about Jesus. He has heard the good and miraculous things Jesus had been doing. He knew he should talk to Jesus to find the answer to life's question. So he went to Jesus and had a dialogue with him.

In our world today, we have very many who shares the same dilemma as Nicodemus. We have people who are very religious and who take their religion seriously. They can be very active and consistent in practicing what they believe. However, they are sensing an emptiness in their lives. There is something missing. They probably don't even know what that missing piece is. And so they are left with a feeling of anxiety. Something is evading them and they can't fathom what it is.

It is for this same reason that people pursue things like wealth, fame and the likes. But when they achieve them, they realize that they are not satisfied. They will want to get more of it or something else. Void, void and more void, never satisfied in these endless pursuits. Be it religion or fame or wealth.

The reason why they are not satisfied is because in all of us, there is a place God prepared for Himself. A place in us that He must occupy. And until God is in that place in us, all pursuits are unsatisfactory. Nicodemus was at that point in his life. He sensed the emptiness, the vacuum or void within him and that made him restless. He had been doing all that is required of him to fulfil what he knew was right to please God, yet he never felt fulfilled. He felt incomplete.

Yes, every one of us is incomplete until we find God and give Him His rightful place in our lives. When we find God through Christ the bible says we are complete. *"And you have been made complete in Christ, who is the head over every ruler and authority."* Colossians 2:10 (BSB).

I commend Nicodemus because he saw that the rituals and doctrines of the law were not bringing him any closer to being complete. He was quick to notice that there was something missing, something related to God. That was what brought him to Jesus. He knew if anyone knows how to get to God, it will be Jesus Christ. At their meeting, Jesus told him the answer to his questions but he did not understand it. Jesus told him that people who want to see God's kingdom both now and in the future must be born again. That startled him but it also gave him the opportunity to ask the Lord: *"How can someone be born when they are old?"* John 3:4 (NIV) it did not make sense to Nicodemus. He was a grown man. So how could this be? It is impossible for him to go back into his mother's womb and be born. What I imagined was adding to his worrisome mind was the fact that he had some knowledge of the speaker of those words. He had seen Jesus performed miracles, saw how he operated and came to believe every word he had spoken. But this phrase was too hard to understand. Nicodemus didn't walk away because he knew that these were words spoken by the greatest man of all times, Jesus Christ. As confusing as that was for him, Nicodemus knew that Jesus meant every word of that and he, was determined to understand it.

The significance of understanding the concept.

Almost every religion has some beliefs about the hereafter. Religious people believe that there is life after death. Because of this belief, they follow what is prescribed in their religious books. Hoping that somehow they will make it to heaven. The interesting part however, is there are no clear cut directions in these beliefs systems that shows a clear path to heaven. These followers are often left without answers to one life's basic questions concerning life and death. In our world today, we have a variety of religions. Each proclaiming to have been sent by God. Each have their doctrines and books to follow. But more often these people find themselves at cross roads when they attend a funeral. They find themselves faced with a reality check. When someone young or maybe a very famous individual passes away; their uncertainty shows. They are troubled within themselves. They just don't know for sure what will happen to them at death. It is for such reason that it is necessary to understand the significance of the "born again" concept.

In bible times, it was evident from the likes of Nicodemus and other religious figures, that religious practices did not guarantee them life after death. If we dig into scriptures, there is a story of a rich religious ruler. This ruler came to Jesus with the direct question. He wanted to know how he can get eternal life.

> *And a certain ruler asked him, saying, Good Master, what shall I do to inherit eternal life? And Jesus said unto him, Why callest thou me good? none is good, save*

one, that is, God. Thou knowest the commandments, Do not commit adultery, Do not kill, Do not steal, Do not bear false witness, Honour thy father and thy mother.And he said, All these have I kept from my youth up. Now when Jesus heard these things, he said unto him, yet lackest thou one thing: sell all that thou hast, and distribute unto the poor, and thou shalt have treasure in heaven: and come, follow me." Luke 18:18-22

There were some interesting exchanges between Jesus and the ruler in that dialogue. First, notice that he came to Jesus to ask about how to get eternal life. This man had been a devout religious man all throughout his life. So for him to have gone to Jesus to ask that question would mean two things. One, he had seen what Jesus had been doing and had developed some faith in Him. He somehow believes that Jesus will have an answer to the most important question of life. After death, what? Two, he was not convinced his religious beliefs and practices will get him eternal life. If he was confident in them, he will not have come to Jesus. Notice he came and asked Jesus a very direct question. He said *"Good Master, what shall I do to inherit eternal life…" Luke 18:18.*

In Jesus's response, He gave the ruler the opportunity to do a reality check for himself. He had been following the doctrines of his faith since he was young. He had kept the commandments and rituals as was prescribed in them. Jesus did not tell this ruler that keeping the law won't save him, instead he let this young ruler see that for himself. He told him to keep the commandments. The man replied; *"all these have I kept from my youth up"* Luke 18:22. The ruler's response was a desperate cry for the truth. In essence he was saying Lord, I have been doing this since I was a young man and it has not help me. I don't know if I will get eternal life following these laws. Jesus, then told him these wonderful words, *"thou lackest one thing …come follow me."* Jesus was telling this ruler that he lacks the one thing that matters. The one thing that makes all the difference between eternal damnation and eternal life. That one thing was to follow Jesus. If you continue that story, the bible say Jesus pity this young ruler; why? Because he had rejected the only way to salvation. The only bridge that crosses from death to life. *"Jesus saith unto him, I am the way, the truth, and the life: no man cometh unto the Father, but by me."* John 14:6

In our world today, there are many people who are in the same position as this ruler. They will come to the truth but will sadly turn away from it. They will reject the only way to life. The bible says:

> *For in Scripture it says: "See, I lay a stone in Zion, a chosen and precious cornerstone, and the one who trusts in him will never be put to shame. Now to you who believe, this stone is precious. But to those who do not believe, the stone the builders rejected has become the cornerstone," 1 Peter 2:6-7 (NIV)*

Jesus is that stone, He is the tried and proven way to God. Which of the prophets or great men of

God, has risen from the dead never to die again? Which one of them had a virgin birth? Which one of them had very many prophecies about their coming into the world. Which of them is coming again? None but Jesus. There is a reason for that, and the reason is He was chosen by God. Therefore, when anyone rejects Him, he rejects the salvation of God. Such a person does not understand and will walk away from the truth like the young ruler. And will miss out on what he had been trying to gain his whole religious life on earth.

Misunderstanding the phrase "born again."

Since that first time the phrase "born again" was coined, it has been misunderstood, misconstrued and misrepresented throughout ages. Like Nicodemus, most people in the world have heard this phrase and their reactions had varied from one set of people to another. Religious folks, have one definition or the other for it, non-religious folks have their own meaning they attached to it. None of which are close to the real meaning of the "born again" concept.

Personally, I am convinced that there are basically two groups of people that propels this wrong concept. The Christians (born again) and non-Christians. For non-Christians, a person professing to be "born again" is probably someone who had lost their sense of direction in life. Someone who is bored to death, and is missing out on life. To them, a person professing to be born again is one who is in a dire situation, such as poverty and destitution. And that person is only in the movement to escape his or her circumstances; and to find consolation. Non-Christians even think that, "born again" people are amongst those who have done some of the worst human crimes and are in need of God's mercies in their lives.

This misconception has been a hindrance to the spreading of the Gospel. People who are out there thinking they are having the time of their lives would not want to be bothered by the boring life of these so-called Christians. They believe that to be born again is to be subjected to unwanted pressures. To have a set of oppressive rules and regulations that are almost impossible to follow. If you ask people for a definition of the phrase "to be born again," you will hear a string of do's and don'ts attached to their meanings. And these are the people that Christians should reach with the gospel.

Before I became a Christian, I constantly looked at people who called themselves "born again" as being deprived of the goodness and pleasures the world have to offer, especially if they were young. I used to pity them, thinking they were not having fun. I was in the clubs, drinking, smoking and having as many girls as I could possibly have. I clearly remembered one young, very beautiful lady who is now married to a Pastor. This lady would come to my house and minister the gospel of Jesus Christ to me when they were out on evangelism. At that time, I was not born again, not even sure if I would ever be. It hadn't crossed my mind to do so yet. Matter of fact, I was looking forward to her visits so I can preach my own "gospel" to her, which was to convince her to go out with me. She would refuse that proposal gently each time and would start to share God's word again. Thank God she didn't stop. I started going to their church on account of her persistence, even though I didn't quite get what it meant at the time. I was just another person who had not come to terms with the meaning of being born again.

Misrepresenting "born again."

Misrepresenting the concept of being "born again" is the other major issue that is a hindrance to the gospel. This is caused mostly by some of us "born again" Christians. As non-Christians misunderstands what it means to be "born again" so do some Christians misrepresents the concept. This in turn has produced confusion and has further buttress the misconception in the world at large. When anyone is in an organization, a club or any kind of group, they represent that group to the outside world. People who knows nothing about such group, will characterize the group by the actions of its members.

Christians have misrepresented the concept of being born again by how we live. Many of us have pushed non-believers far away by our attitudes. We are parading the streets with the holier than thou attitude and as such turning away many potential believers in the Lord. When we go out to talk to non-believers, our message is that of condemnation. We preach sin and damnation. Calling out people and condemning them and making them feel as if they are the worst type of people living on the earth. People who are burdened with sin and addiction do feel the negative effect of their sin and addiction already. Some are genuinely looking for a way out and here come Mr. or Mrs. born again Christian, laying it all heavily on them. This doesn't do them any good at all, if anything, it pushes them far away from the truth of God's love for them.

Christians are God's representatives on earth and if all we do is to beat down already heavy-laden sinners then that's how they will view God.

When the Pharisees brought the woman caught in adultery to Jesus, He handled the situation in a way that gave the woman hope and a platform for her to strive not to sin again. In biblical times, it was the law to stone to death anyone caught in adultery. So since she was caught in the act, she was supposed to be stoned to death. Imagine how she felt as they pulled her away and brought her to Jesus. They read her charges to Jesus. "*Teacher, this woman was caught in the act of adultery.*" (John 8.4)

They quoted the law which says such a person must be stoned to death. This woman knew who Jesus was therefore must have been terrified. She was standing in front of him, in His holy presence, she felt naked and exposed. In her mind, she had giving up all hope and was waiting for Jesus to give the approval for her death. But instead of a condemnation, Jesus gave her a chance to live. The scripture tells us that Jesus bowed His head down and started writing, not answering the accusers. But when they pressed Him, he asked for them to stone her if any of them is without sin. When they heard that, they all departed, leaving the woman standing alone with Jesus. He asked her for her accusers; she told him they left. They left the scene without condemning her. This woman then heard these lovely words from Jesus; *"Neither do I condemn you go and sin no more"* John 8:11 (NLT). Imagine the joy, imagine the freedom from shame, guilt and embarrassment that this woman felt. One act of kindness, an act of love and forgiveness changed the woman's life forever. Our Lord displayed this for us to see and adopt.

Another example of the holier than thou attitude the Lord gave us is in the parable of the prodigal son (Luke. 15:11-32). In this parable, the emphasis is not so much on the prodigal son as a number of preachers and teachers have portrayed. It was actually about the attitude of the elder brother. This attitude is typical of most of us Christians and it is misrepresenting being "born again."

The story was about a father with his two sons, one is older than the other. One day, the young son came to their father and asked for his inheritance and left the house. While he was out there, he spends all his money and became destitute and was reduced to homelessness. The younger son saw his misery and thought of his father's house. The comfort and security he would have if he gets back and apologize for his wrong doing. The story goes that the young son left his misery behind and started walking toward their house. His father saw him from afar off and was delighted. He ran toward his son, accepted his apologies and threw a welcome party for him. This act of the father angered the older brother. He couldn't come to the house and joined the party for his brother. As far as he was concerned, his brother was not fit to come to the house any longer. He was a disgrace to the family and he wouldn't have it! Like the Pharisees who brought the woman to Jesus, he went on accusing his younger brother to their father. Reminding him how his brother lived a wasteful and embarrassing life. The father had to console him and encouraged him to be glad his brother is alive. Oh, but for the heart of the Father. This father showed kindness to his younger son and brought him back home to the family where he actually belongs. The older brother was self-righteous and couldn't see past his younger brother's short comings. He was supposed to had helped his younger brother be a better man but instead was accusing him.

Christians act like that most times, we forgot that we were once sinners who deserved death like every other sinner. We forgot that a year or so ago, some of us were alcoholics and drug addicts who have been saved by the grace of God. We have forgotten that it is in this grace that our status has changed. It is sad when we have the golden opportunity to show the world the goodness and love of God and we fail. Like the elder brother, we condemn other people. We talk down to them in a condescending manner simply because we have come to experience the grace of God. In His mercy, God has picked us up from our own misery in time past. Some of us Christians, were alcoholics, some drug addicts. I could go down the list, calling prostitutes, swindlers, fornicators and adulterers. We were bound by these habits until the grace of God showed up. Some were even in religion with uncertainties of the hereafter. Blindly following whatever it is their leaders told them. Some of us were indulging in secret societies and occultism. And somehow we heard the gospel, believed in it and got saved. Now we are free of the burdens we once carried. Now we have hope in life; we have a relationship with God and can walk in His authority. So we think we are all that. We are better than others. No we are not. The reason why God brought us out of our own misery is for us to be His mouth piece for others to see and come to Him. That they too be free of their burdens and have the same hope for eternity that we have. But we judge the very people we are supposed to show God's love. We scold them for their way of life. Imagine for one second, if it was the elder brother that first came across his younger brother? He would have scolded him and told him how he had brought disgrace to the family's name. He would have counted all the atrocities and abominations his brother had committed against their father. He would have discouraged him from coming home. The younger brother would have died if it was up to his older brother alone. The security and love he had imagined when he was out there would have all been killed by the elder brother.

Sad to say, Christians act this way in many different ways. A Sunday school teacher who happened to be a mechanic was going to preparatory class in his work attire one day. He boarded the train and *'mistakenly'* sat beside a well-dressed Christian brother. I say mistakenly because my well-dressed brother was probably going to an evening service to go praise God. He does not want anything to soil his nice suit. He is a righteous man. He had found Jesus and was walking with him. In his mind, he has it going for him. He is God's child and that was it. Nothing, unclean should sit beside him and now this mechanic in his work attire sat beside him. It never occurred to him that the mechanic is also a child of God. This brother was visibly annoyed and restless and even let the mechanic know. He was shuffling a lot and moving as far from the ill dressed man beside him as possible. This dressed-up Christian realized that the mechanic is a fellow believer when he took out his Sunday school manual to go over a few things. Suddenly, the dressed-up Christian became very apologetic in that moment. These are the type of incidents that misrepresent born again concept. So had the mechanic not been a Christian, that's the perception he would have had of Christians. Living our lives like that is not a true reflection of Christ and can be repulsive to unbelievers. This in turn can make it difficult to have them see God's love for the world.

Personal Experience.

Many years ago, 1 experienced a Christian displaying the holier than thou towards me. There was a wedding for a Christian couple. The wife happened to be one of my friends. The bride's mother had thrown a party for them and I was one of the DJs. The couple arrived, chatted for a while and was about to leave. It was traditional in our Sierra Leonean culture for married couples to dance to a song played exclusively for them. So I asked them if they would dance to a song as is the tradition. I will never forget the reaction of one of the bride's maids, a born-again Christian. This lady spun around with both arms spread apart, shaking them with a waving motion and shouted, "We don't do that!" That didn't sit quite well with me. I interpreted that as her being condescending toward us. I thought to myself, if that's how the "born again" Christians are, who will like to be like them? But of course that is not what to be born again is all about.

If a good number of Christians had a deeper level of understanding the born-again concept; had learned to live and engage interactively with non-Christians it would have made a huge difference. We would have had a more receptive audience and the misconception would have been very small. We will be hospitable, showing respect and understanding to the non-Christians. The non-Christian will be more open to us, increasing the chances of them understanding our message.

What does it mean to be born again?

To understand what to be born again is all about, let us look at the conversation between Jesus and Nicodemus again. Jesus had told him one must be born again to see the kingdom of God. These words took Nicodemus by surprise and Jesus saw that. He saw that his visitor was lost and he had to make clear what he meant by the phrase "be born again" Jesus then said to him, *"Flesh gives birth to flesh, but the Spirit gives birth to spirit."* (John 3:6)

In essence, Jesus reminded Nicodemus of the basic principle of the world. Since creation, God had established that everything will reproduce after its kind. Flesh will reproduce flesh and spirit will reproduce spirit. He was able to direct Nicodemus to see that he was not talking about a physical but a spiritual birth. This spiritual birth is something that neither Nicodemus nor the rest of the world understood. Jesus had to explain it for Nicodemus to get a clue. His encounter with Jesus lifts up his spiritual mind. He now fully understood that there had been a spiritual birth once before and that is what we will examine next.

In this world today, we have millions of people who like Nicodemus have no clue about the spiritual birth. As we go through the pages of this book, it is my prayer that the good Lord who did it for Nicodemus will open such hearts and minds so that they come to understand the meaning of the spiritual birth. Let us now examine the where and when the first of such birth took place.

****

TWO

The First Birth (Spiritual)

****

In the creation narrative, the Bible tells us that God created man from the dust of the earth. Man was lifeless, just one lump of clay with all body parts. Adam was lifeless and clueless of the surroundings. The Bible says God breathed into man's nostrils and man became a living soul. Right there was the first birth!

"And the Lord God formed man of the dust of the ground, and breath into his nostrils the breath of life; and man became a living soul." Genesis. 2:7

Adam's creation was his birth. After God put all the body parts together, there was no life in it. He came alive when God breath into his nostrils. The breath of God in his nostrils was the first spiritual birth. Adam opened his eyes for the first time, there was that instant bonding between God and Adam, similar to how mothers feel bonded to their babies when they first come into the world.

Adam was introduced to the world around him. He met God Almighty, the righteous God. Adam partook of God's nature. This is all he knew, a spiritual connection so serene, so totally involved. Holiness and righteousness were the established culture and so Adam became a part of it all. It is safe to say that Adam knew nothing good or evil. He was just in God's presence, in awe and admiration of this Great God. So this was the first spiritual birth. Adam was born of the Spirit of God. Until he got tempted and fell, he was a man who understood God's ways. However, when he sinned he died spiritually.

Prior to Adam eating from the forbidden tree, God had warned him not to eat of it. He told him that the day he will eat of the tree in the middle of the garden which is the tree of the knowledge of good and evil he will surely die.

> *And the Lord commanded the man (Adam), saying, of every tree of the garden thou mayest freely eat: But of the tree of the knowledge of good and evil, thou shalt not eat of it: for in the day that thou eatest thereof thou shalt surely die"* Gen. 2:16-17.

If you are familiar with the scriptures you will know that when Adam ate of that tree, he did not die as we understand death. However, Adam died spiritually that instant, the very moment after he ate, he went and hid himself from God. Adam was a man who had been in God's company and found pleasure just basking in His presence. God brought the animals to Adam and he named them. What a fellowship! But now all that was gone, thrown out of the window, Adam now dreaded to meet God; he hid himself from Him.

After the fall, Adam lost the spiritual bond with God. His understanding of God became clouded and distorted. He could not have the same conversation with God as he used to. He was separated from God, Adam died spiritually.

Take the physical death of a loved one as an example. When a loved one dies, we don't have fellowship with them any longer. No matter how close we were, there is no talking or doing things together like it used to be. The corpse is buried far away from you who are alive. It seems like they went into hiding so they could not be found. This is an illustration of the relationship between God and Adam after he sinned. Adam was running away and hiding from God just as the corpse is buried in a faraway, lonely place. Ever since that time, mankind had been walking in that lonely place. Very many people living in this world today are lonely and scared. They are in that lonely place feeling inadequate and uncertain about life. They ask themselves ever so often, what is life? Until man discovers God and have fellowship with Him once again, man will be in that place.

In God's view, there are two sets of people in the world. Those who are alive and those who are dead-and-awake. The bible describes it like this:

> *"For God sent not his Son into the world to condemn the world; but that the world through him might be saved. He that believeth on him is not condemned: but he that believeth not is condemned already, because he hath not believed in the name of the only begotten Son of God. John 3:17-18.*

This scripture is saying when God looks down He sees those of us who believes in His Son and those who do not. The believers are alive (not condemned) and those who do not believe as already dead (condemned). In certain countries like ours, when a man is sentence to death because he had been convicted, his prison jumper is marked with a letter C. That letter is capitalized and bold. This is an indication that, that prisoner is a walking dead man. Natural things of this world do teach spiritual truths. The prisoner who is marked with a C is a symbol of the whole human race. This prisoner was not just chosen and marked with a C, condemning him to death. He committed a crime and was processed in the court of law and found guilty. The bible says, *"...all have sin..."* (See Romans 3:23) and we all know sin is a crime committed against God. We also know that God declares that *"For the wages of sin is death"* (see Romans 6:23), so because you and I have sinned, there is that death sentence hanging over us. Our lives are just like the condemned prisoner who will be killed eventually unless he gets a pardon from the right authorities of his country. In most if not all cases, the head of state. In his condemned state, he is a living dead.

To further explain this living-dead concept, I'll draw attention to the scripture which says here. *"But*

Jesus said unto him, follow me; and let the dead bury their dead" *Mathew.8:22.* One day a man came to Jesus and expressed his desire to follow Him. This man told Jesus that he had to go bury his father first. Then Jesus asked the man to follow Him and to let the dead bury their dead. How can a dead man bury another dead man? You and I know that it is impossible for a dead person to bury another dead person. We also know that if Jesus say something; there is got to be a reason and meaning behind it. In this phrase, Jesus talks about the types of death that is in existence in the world. The spiritual death and the physical death.

The spiritual death is what happened the day Adam sin. God told him the day he eats of the tree he will **surely** die. The spiritual death is the one that separates us from fellowship with God. This death permeates throughout the world from that day till the end of the world. Everyone that is physically born in the world since the fall of Adam is born spiritually dead. So in this dialogue, Jesus was told the man who wants to follow him to let the spiritually dead people who are physically alive go bury the physically dead man.

Expulsion from the Garden

Adam eventually faced God and was driven out of the presence of God, out of his guidance and out of his protections. Just like the corpse that is buried far away from the living, Adam was cast out of God's presence into a lonely place. In that lonely place, he felt anxious, the heart that once knew peace was now afraid. The mind that once understood God's will, now finds it impossible to understand it. As far as God was concerned, Adam was dead. He was not spiritually inclined to God any longer. Sin has become a part of his daily living and because of sin, he was separated from God. This separation from God, is the spiritual death. And this death is hovering over the entire human race starting with Adam's children. This spiritual death necessitates the new spiritual birth referred to as "born again."

Adam's children were born into a world in which the view of God had been distorted. Their world was quite different from Adam's. They were introduced to a world of sin and wickedness. They became partakers of sin because they were sinners by birth as is everyone after them. David declares in the Psalm 51:5, *"Behold I was shaped in iniquity and in sin did my mother conceived me."* (KJV) This world has been polluted since Adam and this has been handed down to us. In this state, there is no relationship between God and man. Man is a living dead in God's eyes.

God's Plan of redemption.

However, God intends to have a relationship with us, in fact that was His reason not to kill Adam physically in the garden of Eden. God intends to save the human race and to have a relationship with us again like he once did with Adam before he sinned. It is

God's will that we return to him. *"He is patient with you, not wanting anyone to perish, but everyone to come to repentance."* 2 Peter. 3:9 (NIV) God made a way out for us to come back to him. He loves and cherishes us. It amazes me how much God loves mankind. He has all the power to do the earth over again. He could have just killed us all. Wipe the world clean and start all over. But He chose not to. Instead He sent Jesus to the world to be the way to come back to Him. *"But God commendeth his love toward us, in that, while we were yet sinners, Christ died for us"*. His death bridges the gap for us. We now have the ability to return to God, to fellowship with Him again. Jesus death has brought about the spiritual bond we once lost in the garden through Adam.

The inception of the second birth.

God has a way of doing things. In the beginning, he created Adam to have a continual relationship with him but Adam failed Him. His failure brought sin, chaos and rebellion toward God, which in turn brought suffering on earth. This sin of Adam caused death to span the whole earth. The entire human race was introduced to a world of sin. But God had always loved us, His love for us has been demonstrated over and over again. His love is so awesome that King David in one place asked "...*what is man, that thou are mindful of him...*" Psalms.8:4. It is this love that God have for us that makes him provide a way for us to come back to him.

According to the Bible, sin entered the world by one man, the first Adam, and sin was taking away by one man, the second Adam, Jesus Christ.

But there is a difference between Adam's sin and God's gracious gift. For sin came by one man, Adam, and brought death to many. But even greater is God's wonderful grace and His gift of forgiveness to many through this other man, Jesus Christ." Romans. 5:15 (NIV)

The above scripture did not only show God's love toward us, it also talks about His justice. In all honesty, we were born innocent little kids with no prior records or offenses toward God. But because this world is polluted we become partakers of the corruption and are found guilty of sin. Sin became our nature at birth. This is so because of Adam's sin. In his Justice God sent another man, the bible calls the second Adam to pay for the sins of the world. The first Adam was formed from the dust of the earth and God breath into his nostrils and he became a living soul. That soul sinned and died. God introduced a second Adam into the world to take care of the sin problem. This man was born of a virgin. In bible times an angel was sent to a virgin called Mary with this message.

And the angel said unto her, Fear not, Mary: for thou hast found favor with God. And, behold, thou shalt conceive in thy womb, and bring forth a son, and shalt call his name JESUS He shall be great, and shall be called the Son of the Highest: and the Lord God shall give unto him the throne of his father David: And he shall reign over the house of Jacob forever; and of his kingdom there shall be no end. Then said Mary unto the angel, how shall this be, seeing I know not a man? And the angel answered and said unto her, The Holy Ghost shall come upon thee, and the power of the Highest shall overshadow thee: therefore, also that holy thing which shall be born of thee shall be called the Son of God." Luke 1:31-35

Notice that these two Adams were born of the Spirit. In the beginning, God breath into the first Adam. And the second Adam(Jesus) was conceived by the Holy Spirit. As stated earlier that breath of God in Adam was the first spiritual birth and the second Spiritual birth was seen in Jesus (the second Adam). These are two significant births, the second one more so than the first. As the scripture says, the first Adam brought death. How, by his works. Adam's work affects us all but in the negative way. It brought death and destruction to the world. On the other hand, Jesus's works brings us everlasting life, peace and prosperity. It brings us hope, a better future and an eternal hope in glory. So to be born again one has to believe in the second Adam who is Jesus, his works and teachings. Jesus, the second Adam, died to fulfill God's righteous requirements for sin. His death recreates the atmosphere in which the first Adam was in before sin. An atmosphere for countless number of children to be born into God's kingdom. *"Very truly I tell you, unless a kernel of wheat falls to the ground and dies, it remains only a single seed. But if it dies, it produces many seeds."* John 12:24 (NIV) As a grain of corn that is buried to the ground dies and produce a lot more corn, so does the death and resurrection of Jesus. Because of His death and resurrection, many children are being born into God's home. When anyone understands this concept and believes it, they are on their way to being born again spiritually.

Living the New Life.

When anyone becomes born again he starts a totally different life. Such a person has to conform to the culture befitting a Christian or a believer in the Lord Jesus. This might sound like a difficult thing to do. How can one who was used to live a certain way change all of a sudden. Let us bear in mind that when anyone accepts and believes in the Lord they are being born into the family of God. Now when a child is born, that child is being introduced to a particular culture, a sect, a norm that is the rule of that locality into which they were born. Let's say one of the TV stations creates a new reality show called "Child Swap." A young baby born in China is swapped for another baby born in Sierra Leone. These two kids will grow up living like the rest of the people in the locality they were raised. The child from Sierra Leone will be speaking Chinese and the Chinese born in China will be speaking a local Sierra Leonean dialect. Why would it be so? It would be so because that is the culture they were introduced to as babies.

For Christians, our locality, our culture, our norms and all that makes us unique comes from heaven. We know heaven is not physically with us on earth. So how do we get to live a heavenly life on earth? By reading the bible. The Bible has all there is for us to live according to our new life and position as children of God. In Romans the Apostle Paul said we should not conform to the pattern of this world but we should be transformed by the renewing of our minds. *"And be not conformed to this world: but be ye transformed by the renewing of your mind, that ye may prove what is that good, and acceptable and perfect will of God."* Romans 12:1-2. That renewed mind, is one that is set on God, one that have gone through a cultural make over. Is one that understands the perfect will of God for his life.

Missing the Mark of living the new life

A good number of us Christians are missing the mark of living the Christian life. When we get born again we don't engage in bible studies to know how we should live. We begin to allow our minds to feed us on how to really keep up with our new lives. Our minds will feed us with concepts as to how God wants us to live. What laws to obey, what good deeds we should do. All from the imaginations of our own minds. When a man gets born again, his mind is not born again. It is not an automated process. One has to diligently focus on renewing his or her mind. This is where a lot of us fails. We don't read, meditate or study the scriptures yet we have to live godly. Since we do not read and have no understanding on what to do in a giving situations we let our minds feed us. Some of the things we think about and do are good. But how pleasing are they to God. Once, I was teaching on grace according to Ephesians. 2:8 "For by grace ye are saved…not of works lest any man should boast."

During my teaching, one of my students said, "But there are some sin that you have to punish your body, when you commit them." There is nowhere in the Bible that says so. The trouble with her thinking and so many of us who had accepted Christ as our Lord and personal savior; is that we don't renew our mindset with God's word. In her mind that is a justifiable reason. Sin is categorized and as such it seems right for her to punish her body for a particular sin. That is what I call the gospel according to "you." This means people allow their own minds to tell them what God will like them to do. They don't read the scriptures but follow their own mind. Scriptures says *"There is a way that appears to be right, but in the end it leads to death." Proverbs 14:12 (NLT)* Those of us who are guilty or fall in this category are the ones who are sending the wrong message and are a hindrance to the spread of the gospel. What we need to do is make up our minds and be the Christian God wants us to be. Spend time with God, in our morning devotions, reading the Word and build up our faith. Keeping our eyes on Jesus who is the author and finisher of our faith.

A Pattern to Copy.

The apostle Paul was a religious man who had opposed Jesus until he met him. He was a strongly opposing the gospel of Jesus. But after he met Him on the road to Damascus, his life changed. Paul became a fervent believer in the Lord Jesus. Through his life and ministry, he had left a blue print for us Christians to run a successful race. This man called Paul, was in the same group of religious believers as Nicodemus, he was fighting against believers of the gospel of Jesus. He was doing everything he can to stop them from spreading the good news. At that time, Paul did not believe that the gospel was true so he killed Christians. Threw them in Jail for preaching Christ. All in a bid to stop the spread of what he thought was false. One day, Jesus appeared unto him as he was going on another mission to put the Christians in Jail. At that encounter, Paul became born again. This man shows us a pattern to live a victorious life in Christ. After he had that experience of meeting the Lord on the road to Damascus, he was determined to live for Christ. Paul wrote in his letters to Galatian church this blue print. *"I am crucified with Christ: nevertheless, I live; yet not I, but Christ liveth in me: and the life which I now live in the flesh I live by the faith of the Son of God, who loved me, and gave himself for me." Galatians 2:20*

I would like to break this scripture down to segments for an in-depth explanation so when we grasp the concept, we are on our way to a very successful Christian living. I will draw our attention to the fact that we still live in this world. A world of temptations where we can easily fall or slide back to the things we use to do. But if we grasp Paul's truth we are on the victory track. First Paul declared his state of being. He was crucified with Christ, that was a reminder to himself that Christ died for sin and therefore he should not meddle with sin anymore. The next sentences in that scripture explains how Paul was able to accomplish that. He said, *"it is no longer I (Paul) that lives but Christ lives in me" (See Galatians 2:20b).* Here Paul was saying that, all he had known as the man Paul, all his thoughts of how he can please God. And all how he had learned to interact with his fellow man stopped when he met Christ. He no longer relied on his ability to do those things because Paul has stopped living. And Christ lives in him. Then he said, the life I live, I live by faith in the Son of God. Here is an important lesson Paul learnt and one we should adapt too. Earlier he said he no longer lives and now he said the life he lives, he lives by faith in the Son of God. Paul is expressing the fact that when Christ, is in you, when the Holy Spirit is in you, you are not possessed! Possession will mean, you don't have the ability to use your mind. Your mind will be controlled and manipulated if it were possessed. So Paul was saying the way he lived his own life as Paul, he lived by simply believing and consciously obeying what Jesus tells him to do from his Word.

Consequently, this is an important lesson to grasp. Because sometimes, new converts or even mature Christians do get carried away with misguided ideologies. I had on a couple of occasions led to believe that after I got baptized by immersion, life will change dramatically. So I was excited, counting the days when I will become this super Christian, but the reality was I did not become that super Christian. I felt a little disappointed but was still holding on. I questioned that amongst the brethren The answer I got was another hope raising advice. I will get better when I get the baptism of the Holy Spirit. I did get baptized but I didn't see the drastic change. I learned the hard way that I am a real participant in working my salvation. So Paul's blue print is an eye opener. When a new convert follows this blue print, he is on his way to a victorious Christian living. Instead of living by the gospel according to "you."

To follow Paul's blue print, one should first of all know the word of God thoroughly, read, meditate and study it. Secondly, one should consciously make a choice to live every day for Christ. Interacting with God and man as Jesus prescribes it in the Bible and not by one's own dictates. One should die to self and give in to the Spirit's leading. Remember, the Spirit of God does not possess, He indwells. He counsels, warns but does not decide for you. It will be your decision to follow what the Bible says.

This blue print is full proof, it has proven to work for Paul himself and for many who follow it. At the end of his ministry, Paul said, *"I have fought a good fight, I have finished my course, I have kept the faith." 2 Timothy 4:7* As believers, born again by God's Spirit, let us stay on course and the victory is ours.

THREE

Benefits of Being Born Again.

When a child is born, he or she is entitled to the benefits that are provided by the laws of the land in which he or she is born. One such benefit is obtaining citizenship of that country and having their names recorded in the birth records of the country. If a child is born in America, that child become an American citizen. There will be a record of the date and time of his or her birth and a certificate will be giving to the parents. That is a seal, a confirmation that, that child belongs to America. And as such have rights to all that America provides for her citizens. As like the birth of a child on earth so it is when someone gets born again. Remember when one gets born again, they are born into the family of God and are entitled to citizenship in heaven. And their names will be written in the book of life.

Citizens of Heaven Revealed.

> *Remember that at that time you were separate from Christ, excluded from citizenship in Israel and foreigners to the covenants of the promise, without hope and without God in the world.* ***But now in Christ Jesus you who once were far away have been brought near by the blood of Christ... Consequently, you are no longer foreigners and strangers, but fellow citizens with God's people and also members of his household."*** Ephesians 2:12-13 & 19A ***(emphasis added)***

A member of God's household and a citizen with God's people. This is all part of the benefits to enjoy when one is born again. You have a full proof system, God as the Father of the house, the ruler of His Kingdom. There is no pain or tears shedding in His kingdom because He is a loving and just God.

We all know that we have no abiding city in this world. We know someday we will leave it behind. Better yet, believers in the Lord, knows we are citizens of heaven. Jesus once said, he will go to prepare a place for us! He promised to come again to take us and to live with us in our new heavenly home.

> *In my Father's house are many mansions: if it were not so, I would have told you. I go to prepare a place for you. And if I go and prepare a place for you, I will come again, and receive you unto myself; that where I am, there ye may be also."* John 14:2

Any day now this promise will be fulfilled. Jesus will come down from heaven and those of us who are born again will be taken from this world.

> *For the Lord himself shall descend from heaven with a shout, with the voice of the archangel, and with the*

trumpet of God: and the dead in Christ shall rise first: Then we which are alive and remain shall be caught up together with them in the clouds, to meet the Lord in the air: and so shall we ever be with the Lord." 1Thessalonians 4:16-17

The Marriage Supper of the Lamb

When we go up to heaven, there will a super table dressed for us. This supper is not like the last supper. The last supper brought sorrows because our Lord had to go to the cross and die. But this supper is one of a reunion of the saints. What a day that would be! *"9 And he saith unto me, Write, Blessed are they which are called unto the marriage supper of the Lamb. And he saith unto me, these are the true sayings of God."* Revelation 19:9 (KJV) There will be a gathering of the saints. Both old and new testament saints. What a reunion, what a fellowship that will be. To crown it all, our Lord and Savior, our Master Himself will be there! And of course our loving Father, the Almighty God will there. What a fellowship! Why will anyone want to miss out on this. ***The end of this world and the beginning of the new era.***

This world as we know will come to an end one day. At the end of time, the Bible says, there will be a gathering at the white throne Judgment of God. A gathering of every tribe, nation and kindred that have ever lived in the world. I picture this scene like people coming to America from all over the world and have to go through an immigration port of entry. Amongst the people in the gathering will be citizens of America. The citizens will have a separate line from the rest of the world and they will be allowed to enter the country. At the end of time when all nations, tribes and kindred appear before the throne of God the Bible says, the books are open and another book is open which is the book of life. If any man's name was not found in the book of life, he will be thrown into the lake of fire.

And I saw the dead, great and small, standing before the throne, and books were opened. Another book was opened, which is the book of life. The dead were judged according to what they had done as recorded in the books Anyone whose name was not found written in the book of life was thrown into the lake of fire." Revelations. 20:12&15.

Remember everyone that is born again have their names written in the book of life. This book of life is the birth record of all the children that are being born again by the Spirit of God. Those who believe in Jesus's death and resurrection and those who accepted Him as their Lord and savior. Each time one sinner comes to realize they need a new spiritual birth and they turn to God through Jesus, their names are written down in the book of life. This is the assurance we have as born again Christians. We are born into the family of God and are therefore citizens of heaven. At the final hour, when this world would have been destroyed.

A new heaven and new earth will be ushered in. And this will be our home. "*Nevertheless we, according to his promise, look for new heavens and a new earth, wherein dwelleth righteousness.* 2nd Peter 3:13. The Bible assured us of this eternal life; In his letters to the church, the apostle John wrote, "*I write this to you who have believed in the Son of God, for you to know that you have eternal life.* 1 John 5:13 (NIV)

What I love about this promise, is that it also adds to the uniqueness of the Bible. Now a host of religious believers anticipating to go to heaven; are hoping without assurance. They are teaching people to do good, hoping that the good deeds surpass the bad. But ask one very religious man or woman how many bad or good deeds he or she has done for a day, they don't know. For the born-again believers, that's the assurance we have. Bible says, I write these things so that you may know that you have everlasting life! Hallelujah!

Seeing the world through God's lenses.

Another thing Born again Christians are benefiting is the ability to see the world the same way God does. When God looks at the world, He sees a totally different situation that men do. Men see people who are rich and famous. People who are poor, desperate and needy and average people, to give a rough perspective. From God's perspective, He sees spiritually depraved people, He sees a great number of living-dead people. We can find a classic picture of His views in the bible.

> *The hand of the LORD was upon me, and carried me out in the spirit of the LORD, and set me down in the midst of the valley which was full of bones, And caused me to pass by them round about: and, behold, there were very many in the open valley; and, lo, they were very dry."*
> *Ezekiel 37:1-2*

God saw a valley of very dry bones and if you continue reading God identifies those bones as the entire nation of Israel. Notice that the prophet Ezekiel said, the hand of the Lord was upon him and carried him in the Spirit. Because he was in that state, he was able to see from God's point of view. So just as Ezekiel was able to see the world so can we now. Born again Christians are born of the Spirit and can perceive spiritually. We can now behold the state of the world and this is to spur us to action.

We can now see a world our Lord Jesus looked upon and had compassion. Compassion because the people in the world go after things that are of no benefit to them. He sees a world consuming herself with hate and envy. Jealousy and pride, people just drifting aimlessly. This is the what we are now able to see. The bible says, Jesus saw the crowds, as harassed and helpless like a sheep without a shepherd. This view helps spur us to act against time. Don't people feel good when they do something good for someone who can't help themselves? It is always a good feeling doing so. So when Christians get someone to see and understands their need for Jesus and accepts Him, it is priceless.

God's Provisions to live the life successfully.

Every child born into this world have a father and it is the duty of the father to ensure that there is provision for the child's well-being. He will make sure that from infancy to teenage years even to adulthood there are all the necessities the child will need. Our heavenly Father has done everything to ensure we have a victorious, satisfactory life here on earth.

> *By his divine power, God has given us everything we need to live a godly life. We have received all of this by coming to know him, the one who called us to himself by means of his marvelous glory and excellence."* 2 Peter 1:3

This means, from childhood till adulthood or maturity in our faith, the Good Lord has provided all that we need. We have the Word of God given for our knowledge of him to grow. We have Jesus who is still standing and making intercessions for us and we have the Holy Spirit, who is our Teacher and Comforter. With these resources that are available to believers, we are able to live through this land victoriously. We start as new following The Apostle Peter's admonition. *"As newborn babes, desire the sincere milk of the word, that ye may grow thereby."* 1 Peter 2:2

New Christians should read the word of God and become thoroughly conversant with it. Doing this feeds their spirit man. As we grow up in our spiritual lives as born again Christians, we begin to understand the love God really have for us. We now have a relationship with the Father and can worship Him. We are no longer scared to be in His presence. Bible says *"God is a spirit and they that worship Him must worship Him in spirit and in truth"* John 4:24. Remember Adam was not able to be in God's presence when he sinned. Now because of Christ's work we can now be in God's presence and have talk, and fellowship and live in his presence.

Ability to discern spiritual things.

In God's package, there is the spirit to discern spiritual things. The born again Christian can understands the things of the Spirit of God. We live in a spiritual world and is therefore necessary to discern spiritual things. The scriptures talk of how we must fellowship with the Father. He is a Spirit and we must worship in spirit and truth. Born again believers communicate and comprehend spiritual things unlike the natural man. In Paul's letter to the Corinthian church he talks about the lack of understanding of spiritual things by natural men.

> *The person without the Spirit does not accept the things that come from the Spirit of God but considers them foolishness, and cannot understand them because they are discerned only through the Spirit. The person with the Spirit makes judgments about all things, but such a person is not subject to merely human judgments, for, "Who has known the mind of the Lord so as to instruct*

him?" But we have the mind of Christ." 1 Corinthians 2:14 (NIV)

Who is the natural man? He is the one who has not yet understood the born again concept. Whose understanding of God is either from his own mind or from religious teachings he had received. The Bible says the man without the spirit cannot understand the things of the Spirit. *"God is a Spirit and they that worship Him, must worship Him in Spirit and in truth."* John 4:24

If the bible says, God must be worship in spirit and it also says the natural man cannot understand the things of the spirit, it means there can be no conversation between God and the natural man. The natural man can never communicate with God, simply because they can't understand Him. His language is spiritual. His spirit mind has not yet seen or understand God. The sin issue is yet to be dealt with for him.

In the Gospel of John chapter 6, our Lord Jesus was talking to a multitude of people whom he had fed with five loaves and two fishes. He spoke of the mana the forefathers ate and died. He also told them he is the bread of life and that bread was his flesh. He said "*Very truly I tell you, unless you eat the flesh of the Son of Man and drink his blood, you have no life in you*" John 6:53 (NIV). Upon hearing that many of His disciples left him and never walked with him again. They said that was a hard teaching and they couldn't accept it. Why did they leave? They are natural men; they did not understand what Jesus was saying to them. But when the Lord asked Peter if he was leaving too, Peter answered that Jesus has the very words of eternal life. Where would he go? Peter was spiritual and he understood.

"*The Spirit gives life; the flesh counts for nothing. The words I have spoken to you — they are full of the Spirit and life*" John 6:63. These disciples left because they did not understand spiritual things, their minds were not renewed, they were not a part of God's children. They are natural so they think naturally. Today, many people read the same words of the Bible but it is not profitable to them as yet, and until they become born again, the words of the Bible will not affect their lives as it should because such people read the bible from a natural point of view.

FOUR

Our Mission

****

God has a mission and that mission is to convert the world back to Himself. It is God's will that all men should come to repentance. That all should come to the saving knowledge of our Lord Jesus Christ. This mission of God becomes our mission. Remember, born again believers now see the world from God's perspective. We see people hurting emotionally, physically and mentally. We see a world dying, a world being taking advantage of by the enemy. People loved and cherished by God being played by the devil. We have the responsibility to spread the gospel. God had called us and set us apart and now He is sending us to seek His interest in this world. In 2 Corinthians 5:18-20, the Bible says,

> *And all of this is a gift from God, who brought us back to himself through Christ. And God has given us this task of reconciling people to him. For God was in Christ, reconciling the world to himself, no longer counting people's sins against them. And he gave us this wonderful message of reconciliation. We are therefore Christ's ambassadors, as though God were making his appeal through us. We implore you on Christ's behalf: Be reconciled to God."*

Ambassadors are people who reside in a foreign land to represent and promote the interests of their own country. Now we who are born again believers have the full knowledge that we are fellow citizens in God's kingdom. And we are being sent out as ambassadors representing God's kingdom on earth. God gave us the word of reconciliation which is the

Gospel of Jesus Christ. God knows no one is better to spread this good news than people who have tasted and are enjoying the benefits of being born again.

Our Lord Jesus, after He had trained His disciples and was about to leave the earth, gave them this commission which we call the great commission. And then he told them, *"Go into all the world and preach the Good News to everyone. Anyone who believes and is baptized will be saved. But anyone who refuses to believe will be condemned."* Mark16:15-16

When anyone who becomes born again takes these steps, he will be a very powerful worker in God's vineyard. The Gospel has power to change people, from the gutter most to the upper most, from bondage to freedom. The Apostle Paul said, *"I am not ashamed of the Gospel for it is the power of God to save"* Romans 1:16. Furthermore, in the book of Acts 26:17-18, the Lord told the Apostle Paul *"...I am sending you to open their eyes and to turn them from darkness to light and from the power of satan to God, so that they may receive forgiveness of sins and a place among those who are sanctified by faith in me* (Jesus)." The disciples including Paul did their fair share of spreading this news. They have committed this same word of reconciliation God gave to us all by their examples and now it is here for us to emulate. Copy them and do our fair share.

One important thing I should not leave out of this book is this: In preparing to spread the good news, we have to study. Bible says, *"Study to show thyself approve, a workman that needed not be ashamed rightly dividing the Word of Truth."* 2 Timothy 2:15 (KJV) We should pray and be filled with the Holy Spirit so we can constantly see the plight of the world we are living in, the world we are called to evangelize. The Bible says, when Jesus saw the crowds, he had pity on them because they look like sheep without a shepherd.

The prophet Ezekiel saw a valley of bones, dried up bones. Bones that are not even connected, scattered from each other and are very dried. When God looks down from heaven he sees dry bones. In his conversation with the prophet, God told him that those dry bones were the entire house of Israel. That is the spiritual status of the world in which we live. So God has sent us to see from His perspective and to let this motivates us to speak to the bones. God told Ezekiel to prophesy to the bones, and He is saying the same things to us Christians, preach. At Ezekiel's prophecy the bones came together and flesh came upon them and he breathed on them and they became alive again. A mighty army for the Lord!

When we pray, we will see the same picture, men, women and children in dire need of a savior. Some of them don't even know they need a savior but are very much aware of their plight. Their anxieties, their fears, their unhappiness and miseries. They are looking for a way out. God has given to us the Word of reconciliation, the Gospel of truth. Let us go out and win souls for the Master. Remember whosoever win souls is wise!

****

A Word from My Heart

****

My personal appeal to all of you who read this book. I will like to first address all my fellow believers in the Lord. Whose destiny is certain, who have been made whole by the blood of the Jesus. You are born again! Glory to God. I want to admonish that it is the heart beat of God that we go out and share the good news of His son. Even though we know that, it is necessary that we get reminders from time to time. I want to remind us that we are in the last days. And this is evident in almost every day now. Let's go out, let us hit the streets, the byways, and the highways. Let us cultivate the attitude of our Master. Paul said, let this mind be in you.... what mind?

The mind of Christ. He lowered Himself and went to the cross for us. Suffering from the opposing force but He prayed for them.

Let us not go on a condemnation spree as that hinders the gospel. The more souls that we can win to the Lord, the more we make the world a better place to live. So take up your cross, go to the fields and toil for the Master. Remember, he is coming again soon with our rewards.

Now to the rest of you who are yet to be born again. You may be a very serious religious person. I would like to ask that you do a deep soul searching. Ask God's help. You and I know there are a variety of religions and sects in each of these religions. Each claiming to be God's truth. You know that there can be only one truth. It is important that you seek after and take hold of that truth. The man who is the center of the words "born again" was a religious man like you. He was not satisfied with what he had so he went seeking. Seeking after what? After the truth. God said,

"You will seek Me and find Me when you search for Me with all your heart." Jerimiah 29:13 There was Cornelius another religious man he too because of the sincerity of his heart, found Jesus. Take an inventory of Jesus' life, His birth, His life on earth, His ministry. If those don't do anything for you, consider this. Jesus claimed that he is the ONLY way to God. He is the only one that died and came back from the dead with death having no more hold on Him. Jesus said he came down from heaven and he had returned to heaven. He will be coming again to take all who believed in Him to heaven with him as I wrote in the book. Here is something logical. If you need to ask for direction, and you see a hundred people in a plain field. But ninety-nine of them are dead and there is one alive. Who will you ask for direction? Jesus is alive, all others are dead. There is a heaven to gain and a hell to shun. "For God so love the world that he gave His only begotten Son, that whosoever believes in Him should not perish but have everlasting life." John 3:16.

If the content of this book, opened your eyes and you believe in the work of the second Adam, (Jesus). You believe He died for your sins and would like to express your faith in Him. Accepting Him as your Lord and personal savior. Please pray this prayer.

Father, God I thank you for your word. I believe in the work of your Son Jesus. I believe He died for my sins. I confess my sins to you Father and I am asking that you forgive me. I accept you Lord Jesus. Come into my heart be my Lord and Savior. Thank you, Father, in Jesus' name I pray. Amen. If you pray that prayer, please find a Bible believing church. Where the Born-Again concept is preached. God bless you.